Four Stars
from the
World of Sports

Henry Aaron
Roger Staubach
Kareem Abdul Jabbar
Bobby Orr

by CLARE and FRANK GAULT

Drawings by Ted Burwell

WALKER AND COMPANY
NEW YORK

Contents

Henry Aaron

Henry (Hank) Aaron

THE very first time Henry Aaron left his home in Mobile, Alabama, he was 18 years old. He didn't look as old as 18. He looked more like 15. His face was round like a baby's and he seemed shy.

But there he was at the train station, on his way to join the Indianapolis Clowns of the Negro American League. The Clowns were at their spring-training camp in Winston-Salem, North Carolina. It was the first big step in Henry Aaron's professional baseball career.

Henry's father, mother, his older brother Herbert, sisters Sarah and Gloria were at the station to see him off. Brothers Tommie and James and sister Alfredia were still very young and stayed home with a neighbor.

"Good luck, Henry," said his father.

His mother kissed him. "Take care of yourself," she said.

Henry got on the train. He had his baseball glove and some new clothes in his new suitcase. He had two dollars in his pocket.

Henry's parents were unhappy to see him go. His father wanted him to continue his education. Henry had just finished high school and had turned down an athletic scholarship to a college in Florida. His mother just didn't want Henry to leave home. She didn't think he was old enough to be out on his own.

But Henry was excited. He was going to do what he liked best in the whole world. He was going to play baseball, and for a real professional team. His salary would be small, but Henry didn't mind. He probably would have played for nothing.

In a few minutes, the train moved away. His family seemed to get smaller. Then, he could hardly see the station.

Henry stopped waving and settled down in his straight-backed coach seat. He looked around him. And suddenly, he was scared. He was on his way to a place hundreds of miles away where he had no friends, no relatives. He felt all alone among strangers.

Henry felt homesick already. How did he get himself into such a spot? As he sat there, he thought back to earlier years.

As long as Henry could remember, he wanted to play baseball. He liked all sports. He lived sports, read sports, dreamed sports. In high school, he played end and halfback on the football team. In fact, he was leading scorer one year and had been offered the college scholarship to play football.

But baseball was the game he loved best. He played every chance he got. If there were only a few players around, they played "move up." If only two, they played catch.

And if Henry was all by himself, he played a game in the street that he made up. Using a broom handle and soda-pop bottle caps, he would practice hitting. He had boundaries marked off. To the fire hydrant was a single. Past the neighbor's driveway was a double. All the way to the corner was a home run. But if he hit a bottle cap poorly, it was an out. He had his game marked out under a streetlight so he could even practice at night.

No doubt about it, baseball was his game. He smiled as he remembered one Saturday two years earlier.

"You can't play baseball until your chores are done," his father said. "You and Herbert have a lot of wood to cut."

Henry and his brother, Herbert, had to cut wood for the stove. They made separate piles to keep from having arguments about a fair share of the work.

Henry looked at his tiny pile of cut wood. Then he looked at the pile of wood to be chopped.

"Man," he thought, "there's a lot of work."

Then he looked at Herbert's pile. It was in much better shape. And Herbert wasn't around. So, when his father left, Henry moved some of the cut wood out of Herbert's pile and into his own. "Now, that looks better," he said. Then he left to play baseball with his friend Norman Jackson.

He got to Norman's house.

"Come on," said Henry, "let's play some baseball."

"Can't," replied Norman. "I've got to clean out the garage."

"I'll help you," said Henry.

So Henry pitched in, and worked hard for two hours so that his friend, Norman, could get off to play baseball. But Henry didn't mind the work. He would do almost anything to get up a game.

His high school didn't have a regular hardball team. Softball was played in the school yard. So Henry played softball at school. He pitched, played outfield, infield, wherever a player was needed.

While he was still in high school, he started playing hardball in the local Recreation Department League on weekends. Ed Scott saw him play and noticed that Henry had talent. He asked Henry to join his semi-pro team, the Mobile Black Bears. The summer before his senior year, Henry played regularly with the Bears and earned a few dollars on weekends.

On the last Sunday of the season, the Indianapolis Clowns of the Negro American League came through Mobile on a barnstorming tour. Like most professional teams, the Clowns would pick up extra money by visiting cities outside their own league. They would play the local team and hope to draw a crowd.

Henry played that Sunday. The Clowns' manager was impressed by his hitting and fielding.

"How'd you like to play for the Clowns?" the manager asked Henry.

"I sure would," Henry replied.

"Good. I'll send you a contract."

For months, Henry waited and wondered. Finally, that next spring, a contract for a try-out arrived in the mail. And now he was on his way.

The train trip to Winston-Salem took over 16 hours. It had been warm when Henry left Mobile, but as the train climbed into the Blue Ridge Mountains, it began to get chilly. When Henry got to Winston-Salem, the temperature was in the mid-'40's. Henry was cold. He hadn't planned on 40-degree weather.

Henry reported to the Clowns' training field. The coach grunted and looked

Henry over. He didn't seem very happy to see him. "OK," he said, "follow me."

The coach led Henry to a large room. At one side were lots of bunk-beds. "You can sleep in that one." He pointed to one in the corner. "Breakfast is at 6:30 A.M. If you miss it, you go hungry."

Henry put his few things away in a locker near his bunk. Then he waited.

After a while, the team came in from the practice field. They came laughing, talking and throwing friendly insults at each other. No one paid any attention to Henry as he sat on the edge of his bunk.

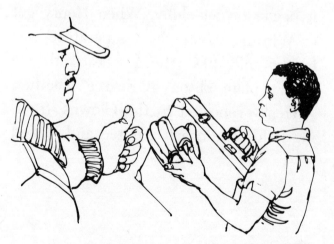

Later, they sat down at a long table for supper. Henry shyly sat at the end and ate quietly. Twice he tried to start talking to the man next to him. But the man just grunted, nodded his head, and turned away.

That night, Henry went to bed very early. He felt alone, and lonely.

Next morning, Henry joined the practice sessions. He had no jacket and it was still cold. He had to keep moving around to stay warm. But no one would throw him a baseball, and he only got a very short batting practice. That night Henry wrote home. He missed his family and he was a little discouraged.

Several days passed. And Henry became even more discouraged. He felt like an outcast. He wondered if he'd get any chance to show what he could do. Then he got a letter from his brother, Herbert. "No matter how discouraged you get," the letter said, "stick with it until they either take you or leave you. You'll never forgive yourself if you don't." Henry agreed that was right. And he made up his mind to stick it out.

A few days later, the Clowns began playing games with other teams training in the area. Henry sat on the bench.

Then one day, the manager put Henry in to play shortstop. The first two times at bat Henry hit singles, and he made a couple of good plays in the field. Henry was excited. "I showed them," he thought to himself.

But the next day, and for several days after that, Henry was back on the bench. Henry couldn't understand it. He had done well and yet no one seemed to take any notice. Again, he felt discouraged.

Now the team was at their home field in Indianapolis, Indiana. And suddenly, Henry saw his name in the line-up again. That day, he got four hits in four times at bat. Again, Henry was excited. And this time the manager did notice. The next day and those following, Henry was in the line-up. He had made the team.

Playing for the Clowns wasn't easy, however. The team traveled a lot, mostly by bus. And sometimes they would play three games in a single day. Often, the ball team would sleep on the bus while riding between cities. But Henry didn't mind. He was playing baseball as a regular, and he was on a hitting spree. In a short time, he was leading the Negro American League, hitting at a .467 average — almost one hit for every two times at bat.

The year was 1952. And one of the best ways for a team like the Clowns to make money was to find a promising young player, train him, then sell him to another team. Henry looked like an up-and-coming player, so the Clowns' owner wrote to several major league teams he thought might be interested. One of them was the Braves, then of Milwaukee, Wisconsin.

When the Braves heard about the teenage shortstop who was hitting over .400, they were interested. They sent a scout, Dewey Griggs, to take a look.

Griggs didn't let anyone know he was coming. He just bought a ticket and sat in the stands like an ordinary fan. That day, Henry got seven hits in eight times at bat. One was a low outside pitch he hit over the right field fence for a home run. Another was a high inside pitch he hit over the left field fence, also a homer. And another was a bunt he beat out for a single.

Griggs was really impressed. But he

noticed something odd about the way Henry swung his bat. Henry held the bat cross-handed. A right-handed batter normally has his right hand above his left. But Henry did just the opposite. His left hand was above his right and his wrists crossed.

After the game, Griggs introduced himself. "I see you bat cross-handed," he said. "Why is that?"

"I don't know," answered Henry, "just habit, I guess. I've always batted this way."

"Well, you really make it harder for yourself," Griggs said. "You won't be able to hit inside pitches as well. Besides, it's dangerous. An inside fast ball could crack your wrist."

Henry said he understood that, but hadn't tried to change.

"Tomorrow, do me a favor, will you?" Griggs asked. "Bat the normal way with your right hand on top, and see what happens."

The next day, Henry held his bat the normal way and got three hits. Now Griggs was impressed again. Here was a young man who could really hit the ball. He could listen too, and try to become a better ballplayer, even though he was hitting at a high average. Griggs made an offer to buy Henry for the Braves. Other teams were interested too, but the Braves' offer was accepted.

After just two-and-a-half months with the Clowns, Henry was on a plane — on his way to join the Braves' Class C farm club at Eau Claire, Wisconsin. The plane was small and made many stops. It bumped and tossed with every air pocket. It was the first time Henry had ever been in an airplane, and he was scared.

When he got to Eau Claire, Henry didn't have to wait to prove himself.

They put him right into the line-up. He hit well right away, and after only two weeks, he was named to the all-star team.

Later, another Braves' scout, Billy Southworth, visited Eau Claire and watched him play several games, then wrote a report to the Braves' General Manager, John Quinn. "Aaron is a line-drive hitter. He has very quick wrists and really lashes at the ball. He can hit the long ball too. A very good big league prospect."

Henry wasn't perfect, though. He was still learning. For one thing, he threw the ball sidearm and even underhand. His throws from shortstop often sank before they reached first and bounced in the dirt. When the first baseman wasn't able to catch them, Henry was charged with errors.

But Henry was improving all the time, and he finished out the season at

Eau Claire with a .336 batting average, one hit for every three times at bat. And although he was there for only part of the season, he hit nine home runs, four triples, and 19 doubles. He was voted the league's Most Outstanding Rookie.

The next year, the Braves promoted Henry to the Tars, their Class A team in Jacksonville, Florida. The Tars were in the South Atlantic League, sometimes called the Sally League.

When Henry arrived at spring-training camp, Jacksonville's Manager, Ben Geraghty took Henry aside for a talk. "You and your teammates Felix Mantilla and Horace Garner will be the first black players in this league. You'll be breaking the color line just like Jackie Robinson did in the major leagues. There's a difference, though. This is the South, and our fans have never seen a black player in one of our uniforms before."

Henry made the major leagues in 1954—and started on the way to breaking records. In June, 1972, he tied Willie Mays for home runs (648), and reporters came to interview him in the locker room.

Henry said he understood, and that he would do his best to avoid any trouble that might hurt the team.

Opening day was rough. Some of the fans booed. Others called names. The opposing players tried to get their goat. But Henry, Felix, and Horace just stuck to their business — baseball.

After the game, Geraghty patted the three players on the back. "That's the way to do it. Play good baseball and the fans will come around."

But the next day, and for the entire series of home games that followed, the fans were cold to Henry and the other two black players. Henry was really hitting the ball, but no one was cheering.

When the team went on the road to visit other cities in the league, the boos became louder and the name-calling uglier. At night, the three black players couldn't even stay with the rest of the team. They had to stay in a hotel in another part of town. The first night on the road, they had a visitor. It was Ben Geraghty.

"Just thought I'd drop by to see if you boys are OK," Geraghty said. He was satisfied that they were all right and stayed to have dinner with them at their hotel. Afterwards, they sat and talked baseball for a couple of hours.

All the rest of the road trip, Geraghty made a habit of stopping to see the three players every night, if only for a few minutes. And often he spent the evening with them.

When the road trip was over and the team returned home to Jacksonville, Henry noticed a difference. The fans weren't booing as much. In fact, one day when he hit a home run, he actually heard some cheers. Soon, Henry, Felix, and Horace were hearing almost nothing but cheers. Jacksonville hadn't won a pennant in 48 years, but suddenly the team was in first place and looking like winners.

Henry was hitting the ball, leading the league. In the field, he was playing second base, but having troubles. His error totals also led the league. He wasn't comfortable at second base, and he was making mistakes.

He still had some things to learn about base running too. In one game, he stole second base three times. But he got called out all three times because he strayed off the bag while the second baseman still held the ball.

Toward the end of the season, the Jacksonville team clinched the pennant and Henry was shifted to the outfield. The Braves wanted him to get outfield experience.

Henry finished the season with a .362 batting average, high for the league.

And he was elected Most Valuable Player.

That winter, instead of letting Henry go home for the off-season, the Braves sent him to play winter ball in Puerto Rico. They wanted Henry to get more experience playing the outfield. Henry was glad. It gave him the chance to play more baseball, and it showed that the Braves were interested in his career. Henry felt that he was about to get his chance in the major leagues.

But then the Braves got Bobby Thomson from the New York Giants. And suddenly it looked as if the Braves had all the outfielders they needed for their major league team. The rumor was that Henry was slated for another minor league team, the Braves' Class AAA team in Toledo, Ohio.

Then an accident happened. Bobby

It's a good one! Home run number 700 for Henry Aaron
—July 21, 1973.

Thomson broke an ankle sliding into a base. The next day Braves Manager Charlie Grimm started Henry in left field. They were still in spring training, but Henry knew this was his big chance. That day, Henry got three hits, including a home run that went out of the ball park and over a row of trailers parked along the edge of the field.

"The job is yours," Grimm said.

Henry was 20 years old. He had been playing professional baseball for just two years. And now he was in the major leagues, starting left fielder for the Milwaukee Braves.

Henry was excited and anxious too. He knew that a question hangs over every new player who comes into the major leagues. Can he make it? Henry knew that many players with great minor league records didn't. Would he be able to hit major league pitching? That was the big worry.

The Braves opened the season in Cincinnati. Henry was eager to do well. He felt the pressure. Perhaps the pressure was too great. In five times at bat, Henry went hitless.

For their next game, the Braves went back to their home grounds for a series against the St. Louis Cardinals. Vic Raschi was pitching for St. Louis. His first time at bat, Henry hit the ball off the left center-field fence for a double. Henry had his first major league hit!

Henry was very happy. He almost felt like skipping to second base.

About a week later, Henry got his first home run, along with two other hits in seven times at bat. Henry Aaron was in the big leagues to stay.

That was the beginning of Henry's professional baseball career. He has been one of the most productive players of all time. A home-run hitter, of course.

One of the greatest. But also a hitter of a great many singles and doubles. Only 10 players in the history of baseball have over 3,000 base hits. Henry is one of them. Henry and Willie Mays are the only players to have 3,000 hits and more than 600 home runs.

Back when Henry was hitting pop-bottle caps under the streetlight, he dreamed he was a great hitter in the big leagues. He dreamed it on his ride from Mobile, Albama, to Winston-Salem, North Carolina. For Henry Aaron, dreams do come true.

Henry Aaron's hitting record in professional baseball, 1954-1972

Year	Games played	At bat	Runs	Total hits
1954	122	468	58	131
1955	153	602	105	189
1956	153	609	106	200
1957	151	615	118	198
1958	153	601	109	196
1959	154	629	116	223
1960	153	590	102	172
1961	155	603	115	197
1962	156	592	127	191
1963	161	631	121	201
1964	145	570	103	187
1965	150	570	109	181
1966	158	603	117	168
1967	155	600	113	184
1968	160	606	84	174
1969	147	547	100	164
1970	150	516	103	154
1971	139	495	95	162
1972	129	449	75	119
Totals	2844	10,896	1976	3391

Two-base hits	Three-base hits	Home runs	Runs batted in	Batting average
27	6	13	69	.280
37	9	27	106	.314
34	14	26	92	.328
27	6	44	132	.322
34	4	30	95	.326
46	7	39	123	.355
20	11	40	126	.292
39	10	34	120	.327
28	6	45	128	.323
29	4	44	130	.319
30	2	24	95	.328
40	1	32	89	.318
23	1	44	127	.279
37	3	39	109	.307
33	4	29	86	.287
30	3	44	97	.300
26	1	38	118	.298
22	3	47	118	.327
10	0	34	77	.265
572	95	673	2037	.311

Add in Henry Aaron's 1973 home runs.

How does his total compare to Babe Ruth's total of 714?

Roger Staubach

Roger Staubach

LT. Roger Staubach was about to take an important trip. He was an officer in the U.S. Navy, but he didn't look it. He was dressed in a sports jacket and slacks.

His suitcase was packed and stood in the hallway. A taxicab pulled up in front of the house.

"Good-bye, honey," he said. "Wish me luck."

He kissed his wife. Then he hugged his two little girls. He picked up his suitcase and left. At the curb, he gave a final wave with his hand.

Roger wasn't going to be away for long. Just two weeks. But they were an important two weeks that would help him make a big decision. Should he stay in the Navy? Or should he try for a career playing professional football?

Lt. Roger Staubach was on his way to spend his leave time with the Dallas Cowboys football team at their training camp. At the end of the two weeks, he would make his decision.

Roger still had more than a year on his first hitch with the U.S. Navy. As a graduate of the Naval Academy at Annapolis, he had to spend at least four years on active duty. He sometimes wondered what might have happened if he had gone to school at Notre Dame or Purdue. If he had gone to a regular college, he could have joined a professional football team right out of school.

But Roger had chosen Annapolis. And he was glad he had. In high school, he had been a star quarterback at Purcell High in Cincinnati, Ohio. And many colleges including Notre Dame, Purdue, Ohio State, and Annapolis had all offered him full scholarships. But he had liked the Naval Academy, Annapolis, best.

At Annapolis, Roger tossed pennies to the statue of Indian Chief Tecumseh for good luck. As star quarterback of the Navy, he led the team to many victories.

And Navy had been glad to have Roger on their football team. In 1963, he had led the team to a string of victories that put Navy high in the national ratings. They had been voted the second best team in the United States. That year also, as a junior, Roger had won the Heisman Trophy as the outstanding college football player.

When he was graduated in 1965, the Dallas Cowboys signed Roger to a contract. They knew that Roger would have to spend four years in the Navy before he could play with the team. But they were willing to give him a bonus of $50,000 for signing the contract anyhow. And they would pay him $750 a month salary all the time he was in the Navy. If he decided to stay in the Navy, that was it. He didn't *have* to play football, and he didn't have to return any of the money.

There wasn't any question about Roger liking to play football. Even when he was in Viet Nam he spent a couple of hours every day throwing the football to a former teammate. The question was: Did Roger feel that he was good enough to play? And was he ready to give up his Navy career to try?

After his tour of duty in Viet Nam was finished, Roger was stationed at the air-training base at Pensacola, Florida. Here at least there was a football team. It was not a good one, but it was better than no football team at all. The Pensacola Goshawks were mostly a pick-up team that took whoever was on the base. The moment Roger arrived, he was made starting quarterback and offensive coach.

The Goshawks played small teams, mostly in the South. With Roger at quarterback and coaching, the team won six of eight games. This was a good record. But what did it prove? The teams they played were not top rank.

But now, Roger was on his way to try his hand with the real pros. And that could be a very different story. After all, many a college star hadn't done well in professional football. Even Heisman Trophy winners hadn't.

When Roger arrived at the Dallas training camp at Thousand Oaks, California, he was put with the rookie squad. Two weeks wasn't much time. He had to get into shape. He had to learn some of the difficult Dallas formations. And he had to try to find out if he had a future in football.

Near the end of his two-week stay, Roger got a chance to play with the rookie squad in a scrimmage against the rookies from the San Francisco 49ers. He threw three touchdown passes.

A couple of days later, the Cowboys' rookie squad played the Los Angeles Rams' rookies. Roger completed 13 of 16 passes.

When his two-week leave was over, Roger said good-bye to the team and went home to his family.

"I think I know, now," he said to his wife. "I can make it in professional football. I can, and it's what I want to do."

But Roger knew that breaking into the pros would be a tough battle. He still had another year of Navy service to finish. And the Cowboys already had three experienced pro quarterbacks.

The Cowboys' number-one quarterback was Don Meredith. He had been with the team since it was first formed. He had led them from the years when they had very few victories to times when they won nearly all their games. Twice he led them into games for the championship. Both times they failed to win only by a yard or two.

The Cowboys' second quarterback was Craig Morton. He had been Roger's teammate on the 1965 all-star team. Since then, Craig Morton had been with the Cowboys as second-string quarterback to Don Meredith. All the time Roger was in the Navy, Craig Morton was gaining experience as a professional quarterback.

The Cowboys also had Jerry Rhome, an experienced quarterback who had been in the National Football League for years.

The season that followed training camp Roger learned more about Dallas football by studying a play book that Coach Landry gave to him. And Roger watched Dallas games on TV. He kept in shape by playing with the Pensacola Goshawks again that year.

The next year, Roger got out of the Navy. His four years were over. The summer of 1969, he reported to the Cowboys' training camp. He was 27 years old, four or five years older than most rookies. And he hadn't played any real first-class football in four years.

But things began to happen very fast. First the Cowboys traded Jerry Rhome because they thought they had more quarterbacks than they needed.

And suddenly Don Meredith called it quits. He was only 31 years old, not old for a quarterback. But he felt that he just couldn't hack it anymore. He wanted to take up TV announcing instead. That left Craig Morton and Roger Staubach.

Naturally, Craig Morton was first-string quarterback when training camp opened. And he ran the team through most of the pre-season warm-up games. Then, just two weeks before the opening game of the regular season, Craig Morton was hurt.

The Cowboys were playing an exhibition game with the New York Jets. The game went badly for the Cowboys, and the Jets were ahead 9–3.

Just before the end of the first half, the Cowboys had the ball deep in their own territory. Morton dropped back to pass. He threw the football, but as he let go of the ball, his hand hit the hard helmet of an inrushing lineman. A finger of his throwing hand was sprained.

There was just a little over a minute to play in the first half when Roger was sent into the game. He had worn a Cowboy uniform only a few weeks. And this was his chance to show what he could do.

On the first play, Roger handed the ball to fullback Walt Garrison on a draw play. It gained 11 yards. Then came an incomplete pass. Roger tried to pass again. But he couldn't find an open pass-receiver and was forced to run with the ball. He gained eight yards. Calvin Hill then carried the ball over right tackle for a first down on the Cowboy 43-yard line. Time was running out. There were only 45 seconds left in the first half.

A screen pass to Hill gained 21 yards. Another pass was good for 16 yards. Now the Cowboys were getting close. But only 12 seconds were left. Roger dropped back to pass. Again, he couldn't find an open receiver. He dodged one tackle. Then another. Suddenly, he saw an opening and ran around right end. And he made it into the end zone for a touchdown. There were only four seconds left in the first half.

That was the first time Roger had a chance to lead the Cowboys in a real game. And he had led the team to a touchdown.

In the second half, the Cowboys continued to move the football. And their defense was air-tight. The game ended in a Cowboy victory, 25–9. Roger was very excited. What a wonderful start!

But the next week things didn't go so well. The Cowboys played the Baltimore Colts in another exhibition game. The Colts had one of the toughest defenses in football. Morton was still hurt, so Roger played quarterback.

The big Colt line chased Roger all over the field. Roger gained over 100 yards with his scrambling runs. But his passes were intercepted four times. The Cowboys lost, 23–7.

Morton's finger was getting better, but he still wasn't ready to play in the first regular season game. So Roger had to play. Coach Tom Landry was unhappy. He felt that Roger needed more experience. He didn't mind putting an exhibition game into Roger's hands. But this game was for the record. It really counted.

The game was with the St. Louis Cardinals. It got off to a slow start. Neither team seemed to be able to move the ball. Then, suddenly, Roger dropped back to pass. Lance Rentzel raced downfield. Roger threw a perfect pass. Rentzel caught it and went all the way for a touchdown. The play had covered 75 yards.

Later, in the third quarter, the Cowboys scored again. And then again, when

Roger was forced to run on a messed-up play. When it was all over, the Cowboys had won, 24–3. Roger felt that he had shown his true ability to run the team.

But the next week, Morton was back in action. And Roger was back on the bench. He stayed there for all the rest of the season. Roger got into a few games, but only in the final minutes after the Cowboys had big leads and it didn't matter. Craig Morton did a good solid job, and the Cowboys were champions of their division. But in the play-offs, Dallas lost to the Cleveland Browns in a game where everything seemed to go wrong.

Between seasons Morton had an operation on his arm, and it looked as if he might not be ready to play soon enough. But when the 1970 training camp opened, Morton was the number one quarterback. And Roger was still trying to convince Coach Landry that he should be number one.

Morton led the team through most of the exhibition games. But in the last one, against the Jets, he didn't do well and was replaced by Roger. Roger also got the starting job in the first game of the regular season and led the Cowboys to a 17–7 win over the Philadelphia Eagles.

After that, he led the Cowboys to victory over the New York Giants, 28–10. Roger felt he was on his way. But again, Coach Landry stepped in.

The following week, the coach pulled Roger out of the game after a first-quarter interception and sent Craig Morton in. And even though the Cowboys had some bad games the following weeks, Coach Landry kept Morton on as the first-string quarterback.

After a number of losses, the Cowboys pulled themselves together and started winning again. Craig Morton's

arm was sore and he could hardly throw
the ball. But the Cowboy defense and
running game were great. And they won
their division. In a play-off game with
the Detroit Lions, neither team could
move the ball on offense, but the Cowboys managed to collect a field goal and
a safety for a 5–0 win.

Roger sat on the bench throughout
this entire series of games, still waiting
for a chance. He watched from the side-
lines as the Cowboys just edged past the
San Francisco 49ers for the National

League championship. And he was on the bench during the whole Super Bowl game as the Cowboys lost to the Baltimore Colts in a dismal game.

Roger was a bit discouraged. He had been with the Cowboys two full years and he had started just four games. Roger felt he had done well. But no matter what happened he couldn't seem to win Coach Landry's confidence.

"Well, maybe next year will be different," Roger said to himself.

The next season, 1971, didn't start off any better. Coach Landry seemed to have lost confidence in Craig Morton, but he didn't seem to have gained confidence in Roger. Coach Landry announced that the quarterback job was up for grabs. Then he rotated his two quarterbacks. First, he would start one, then the other. Finally, Coach Landry reached the point where he was changing quarterbacks every quarter and even every few plays.

This new system didn't work very well. The whole team was upset. And after seven games the Cowboys had a season record of four wins, three losses. They were two games behind the Washington Redskins in the race for their division title.

Then one evening during the middle of the week Roger got a phone call. It was Coach Landry. "Roger," he said, "I've reached a decision. You're my starting quarterback."

The big moment Roger had worked and waited for had arrived. Now he didn't know what to say. Finally, he said something about doing his best and hung up.

"At last," Roger told his wife. "At last, I've got the job."

The next week with Roger as first-string quarterback, the Cowboys barely

After two years, Coach Tom Landry (at left) finally gave Roger the job of first-string quarterback of the Dallas Cowboys.

beat the St. Louis Cardinals, 16–13. But in the following weeks they picked up steam. They beat the New York Jets, 52–10 and the New York Giants, 42–14. In the key game with their division rivals, they beat the Washington Redskins, 13–0. And finally, they took the division title by beating St. Louis, 31–12.

In the play-offs, the Cowboys met the Minnesota Vikings and beat them, 20–12. Then came the San Francisco 49ers for the National League championship. In a very hard-fought game, the

Cowboys won, 14–3. And it was really thanks to Roger. His passing and scrambling runs upset the 49er defense and forced them to loosen up their tight coverage of pass receivers.

Now the Cowboys were back in the Super Bowl for a second crack at the title. Their rivals this time were the Miami Dolphins. And the game went differently too. The Cowboys' defense was very tight. And Roger Staubach was at quarterback. That afternoon, Roger completed 12 of 19 passes for 119 yards and gained 18 yards running. Final score of the game: Dallas 24, Miami 3.

Roger had done it! He had made it in professional football, even after a four-year gap caused by his duty with the Navy. He had come back. He had won the job as starting quarterback. And he had led his team to victory in the Super Bowl.

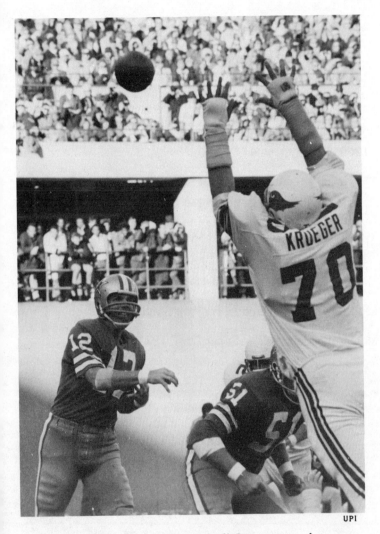

UPI

Roger (Number 12) sends the ball flying over the arms of Rolf Krueger of the St. Louis Cardinals. The Cowboys beat the Cardinals and took the division title in 1971.

Roger Staubach's passing record in professional football
1969-1972

Year	Passes thrown	Passes completed	Percent
1969	47	23	.489
1970	82	44	.537
1971	211	126	.597
*1972	20	9	.450

*Injuries made Roger miss almost the whole 1972 season.

Leading passer — National Football League, 1971

Most Valuable Player — Super Bowl, 1971

Average gain	Total yards	Touchdowns	Interceptions
8.99	421	1	2
6.61	542	2	8
8.92	1882	15	4
4.90	98	0	2

Kareem Abdul Jabbar

Kareem Abdul Jabbar (Lew Alcindor)

LEW Alcindor's life changed a lot when he went into the fourth grade. Up until then, everything was just average. He lived at home with his parents and went to school nearby. He was the only child of the Alcindors, but there were lots of boys to play with in the housing project where he lived.

Lew liked his neighborhood. It was a nice part of Manhattan, New York. Two parks were close by with wide green lawns and plenty of trees.

Lew's family were Catholic, and Lew went to St. Jude's School. He and another boy were the only black children there at that time, but no one seemed to pay any attention to that. He liked school and had many friends there.

Lew's father was a policeman in the New York Subways System, even though he had been graduated from a famous music college. Lew's mother kept house and looked after Lew. But just as Lew was about to go into fourth grade, his mother decided that she would get a job too. Then, things changed. And Lew's parents were worried about his coming home to an empty house after school.

"Lew," his father said, "we've decided to send you away to school next year. We want you to be where you'll be taken care of and we won't have to worry. We're going to send you to Holy Providence School just north of Philadelphia."

Lew didn't like leaving his home and all his friends from St. Jude's and his neighborhood. But he knew that his parents were doing their best for him. So, off to the new school he went. He was nine years old. He looked older than nine because he was five feet four inches tall already. That made him the second tallest boy at Holy Providence. The tallest boy was in eighth grade.

Right away, Lew felt strange at the new school. Not because he was so tall for his age. He was used to that. People had always talked and said funny things about his being tall. He felt strange because Holy Providence wasn't anything like St. Jude's. Nearly all the students at Holy Providence were black.

Most of them came from poor neighborhoods in Philadelphia, Baltimore, and Washington, D.C. And they were tough. They spoke words that Lew had never heard before — words they wouldn't say when the nuns were close enough to hear them. And they talked about things that Lew had never heard about before.

The boys at Holy Providence treated Lew as a stranger. He wasn't like most of the other children. He was quiet. He was polite. And he was a good student.

One day, during English class, the teacher had all the children read aloud. Each one read a few paragraphs in turn. Most of the students stumbled over the words. But when it came Lew's turn, he read his part perfectly.

"My, Lewis," the teacher said, "you read beautifully."

Lew didn't think much about it. He had always read a lot. He liked to read and there were always plenty of books

at home. But the boys at Holy Providence never read, except when they had to in school. Now they really thought Lew was strange.

Later that day, the teacher took Lew to a seventh grade class and had him read aloud again.

"Now, students," the teacher said, "that's the way to read. Lewis is only in the fourth grade, but he knows how."

That night, at supper, Lew was walking with a tray of food when someone stuck out a foot and tripped him. Lew fell flat, food and all. There was gravy on his shirt, and some mashed potatoes too. Everybody laughed and made fun of him.

Later, when Lew tried to climb into bed, he found the sheets had been folded up under the covers so that he couldn't get in. Lew felt bad, and very lonely.

For weeks, the boys played tricks on him and made fun of him. Lew just kept quiet and didn't fight back. How could he? The whole school seemed to be against him.

Then one day a group of boys were standing in the school yard. They were looking him up and down, and whispering.

"I wonder what they're going to do to me now?" Lew said to himself.

"Come on, kid," said one of the boys, "we're going to teach you a game."

The boys had a basketball. They had tied a peach basket up on the crossbar of the playground swings. And they played "school-yard basketball" around and under the single basket. Mostly they played three players against three players. The game was rough and there was no referee. There was lots of pushing and shoving. One player might even trip another. Or bump him hard when he dribbled past.

But Lew didn't mind. He liked the game. And he was excited. For the first time, the other boys made him feel like part of the group.

The boys picked Lew because he was so tall. They thought he would be a natural basketball player. He wasn't.

Lew was tall, but he was also clumsy. He practiced hard with the boys and got better, but when they visited other schools to play on regular courts, Lew mostly sat on the bench. Most of the regular team were eighth-graders, four or five years older than Lew. But Lew could see that being tall would help — if he just weren't so clumsy.

During the year, Lew's parents visited him every chance they got. And Lew went home at Christmas and Easter. His mother and father could see that Lew was not the same boy they had sent away earlier. Lew was careful not to use any of the dirty words he had learned, but they could tell he was tougher. And they didn't like it. So when the school year was over, his parents decided that Lew would go back to St. Jude's in the fall.

In the fifth grade, back at St. Jude's, Lew went out for basketball again. He was even taller. He was clumsier too. His feet got tangled up when he ran. His hands didn't seem to work together. Lew was on the team, but he didn't get much chance to play in the games. His size got him on the team, but Lew could see that he needed more than that. He didn't understand why he was so clumsy and couldn't play better. He just knew he had to do something about it.

All that next summer, Lew ran track — short dashes, then long runs of a mile or two. He got faster, and he also learned to control his feet and legs. He practiced dribbling and shooting several hours each day at the playground basket. His shooting improved and so did his dribbling.

By the sixth grade, Lew was over six feet tall and still growing. But now he was learning how to use his size and he was learning how to control his body. He still felt shy about playing in front of people, though. He was afraid of looking clumsy. His coach, Farrell Hopkins, helped Lew get over that.

"Look, Lewis," Mr. Hopkins said, "the reason you feel shy is because you're afraid you'll miss an easy shot, like a lay-up. These shots are just a matter of practice. Let's work on it."

Mr. Hopkins showed Lew how to use the backboard on lay-ups. He showed him how to make hook shots. He showed him how to increase his chances on jump shots. Mr. Hopkins arranged for Lew to practice alone in the gym for an hour or two every night. When Lew practiced alone, he wasn't afraid of looking clumsy. And after he became sure he could make the shots he wanted, Lew got the confidence to play in front of people.

In seventh grade, Lew reached six feet five inches. Now he played as a regular on the basketball team. One day, at practice, Lew made a big discovery. He jumped up while making a shot and his hand hit the rim of the basket. "Wow," he thought to himself. After practice, he waited until everybody left for home. Then he jumped up and touched the rim thirty times in a row, just to prove that he could really do it.

Something else happened in seventh grade. Racial problems began to trouble Lew. As long as he could remember he had always lived in a mostly white neighborhood. And he was only one of a few blacks at St. Jude's. But until the seventh grade it didn't seem to matter. Nobody paid any attention. He played games with white boys. In fact, for years his best friend was an Irish boy named John. They went everywhere together.

Then one day Lew and John had a small fight. It was no more serious than dozens of others they had had over the years. But this time John acted differently. He got very red in the face and called Lew, "nigger." Later, John and some of his white friends followed Lew home calling him names. Lew couldn't understand.

Then other things happened — small things, but they added up. It seemed to Lew that a wall had come between him and many of his white friends. It wasn't a wall anyone could see, but Lew felt it was there. Lew spent more and more time with his basketball practice, and less time trying to be friends with the neighborhood boys.

St. Jude's was a grade school. It didn't play a big schedule of games. But Lew noticed that coaches from private high schools began showing up at games to watch him play. In eighth grade, Lew was six feet eight inches tall. And he was looking more like a basketball player all the time. He could dunk the ball now, and sometimes he scored thirty points or more in a game. He captured more than his share of the rebounds and made it hard for the other team to score.

Some private high schools wanted Lew for their teams. They offered Lew full scholarships. One of them, Power Memorial Academy, was in Manhattan, only a subway ride from Lew's home. Lew met their coach, Jack Donohue, and liked him. He also liked the school. So Lew decided to go to Power.

Coach Donohue had a fine bunch of basketball players at Power. But having Lew at center really made the team go. In his second year, Lew began to use his size. When the other team ganged up on him, he passed the ball off to Oscar Sanchez or Jackie Bettridge or Bobby Ericson. And if the other team

UPI

Lew leaps for the basket during the Catholic High School AA Championship game in 1965. Power won the game against Rice, and Lew was named Most Valuable Player.

didn't put a couple of players to guard him, Lew would get more than his share of baskets. No one could stop the Power team. They finished the season undefeated and were city champions of all the Catholic schools. Lew averaged 19 points and 18 rebounds per game.

And the Power team kept right on going the next year. One time they were playing Boys' High. Lew was a full head taller than the center of the other team. So, with his greater size Lew just kept leaning over the other boy — keeping the ball away, blocking passes, and taking most of the rebounds. All during the game, the other center kept bumping his head against Lew, getting madder and feeling more and more helpless. Suddenly, Lew felt a terrible pain in his left arm. The other boy had bit him. There were teeth marks deep into the flesh of his arm. The other boy had just lost control of his feelings.

The Power team won game after game. Newspapers and magazines ran stories about the team. Mostly they wrote about Lew. Coach Donohue began trying to tell Lew how to act and what to do off the basketball court. Coach Donohue didn't want Lew to visit Harlem. He was afraid Lew might meet some bad people there. But Harlem was where Lew had black friends, and that's where Lew went to have fun. He felt that Coach Donohue was treating him like a piece of property.

Even though Lew and Coach Donohue had some disagreements, Lew liked and respected his coach. He even spent his summers between school years at Mr. Donohue's day camp in upstate New York. Most of the time he felt warm and friendly toward Mr. Donohue. Then came a real shocker. One night Power was playing a game against St. Helena's of the Bronx. It should have been an easy game for the Power team. But it didn't turn out that way. At half time, Power was ahead by only a few points when they should have been far ahead.

Lew knew that he hadn't played his best and he was disgusted with himself. In the locker room at half time, Coach Donohue scolded his team. Player by player, he pointed out mistakes. Then he pointed to Lew. "And you. You go out there and you don't hustle. You don't move. You don't do any of the things you're supposed to do. You're acting just like a nigger."

Lew was stunned. He felt like walking out of the game right then and there. It wasn't enough to be scolded for his mistakes. He had to be called a nigger too!

Lew went back for the second half, but he was in a daze. He didn't remember much of what happened. Power did better, though. They won the game easily.

After the game, Coach Donohue called Lew aside and said, "See, it worked. I knew if I called you that word, I'd shock you into a good second half. And I did."

But Coach Donohue's explaining didn't make Lew feel any better. Lew thought to himself, "It's no good, Mr. Donohue. It just isn't right."

After his junior year, Lew decided he wouldn't return to Mr. Donohue's day camp. He had always been the only black person there, and he felt shut off from the rest of the boys. Instead, Lew decided to take a job with an organization in Harlem. It was called HARYOU-ACT and its purpose was to help the poor people of Harlem.

Mr. Calloway was teaching Lew his job, and Lew began to learn things about black people that made him feel proud. For example, he learned that there were old civilizations in Ghana and Mali. And that there was an empire in Africa 700 years ago. As soon as he heard about these things, Lew would run to the library and look them up. Sure enough, the facts were there. But no one had taught them in school.

One morning, after a couple of weeks, Mr. Donohue stopped by Lew's home and offered to drive him to work. All the way to Harlem, Mr. Donohue talked to Lew about the day camp. Mr. Donohue was in a spot. He had told the boys attending his camp that Lew would be there for the basketball practices and they were expecting Lew. Lew wanted to stay with HARYOU-ACT, but he agreed to help Mr. Donohue. Lew returned to the day camp.

In Lew's senior year, the Power team

went right on winning. They ran up a string of 71 games before they were finally beaten in a close game by De-Matha Catholic High School of Hyattsville, Maryland. The boys were all sad about losing, but Mr. Donohue tried to make them feel better. He told them that they had played well, and that everybody had to lose sometime.

After they lost to DeMatha, Lew and the other boys picked right up again and started a new winning streak. At the end of his senior year, the Power team had won three straight New York Catholic High School Championships. They had lost only one game in three years. And Lew had scored 2,067 points, a city record.

By now, Lew had nearly reached his full height of seven feet two inches. He was famous. Newspapers and magazines all over the country wrote stories about him. Many colleges wanted Lew for their basketball teams.

Mr. Donohue became famous too. And he received offers to coach for college teams. Finally, he decided to coach at Holy Cross College.

Lew, in the meantime, became interested in UCLA (University of California at Los Angeles). UCLA did everything to get Lew. Ralph Bunche, former Ambassador to the United Nations, wrote Lew. Mr. Bunche had played guard on the UCLA basketball team many years before. Jackie Robinson, who used to play football and baseball for UCLA, also wrote him a letter. In April of his senior year at Power, Lew got an invitation to fly out to Los Angeles to look the university over.

Lew was given a grand tour of UCLA by Mike Warren and Edgar Lacey, stars of the basketball team. He met and liked John Wooden, the basketball coach. And he loved the campus. Warren and Lacey were both black players and they told Lew that UCLA was a great place.

Mr. Donohue asked Lew to visit Holy Cross too. Lew was almost sure that he was going to UCLA, but he agreed to visit Holy Cross. When he got there, Mr. Donohue arranged for a black basketball player to show Lew around.

"Listen to him," Mr. Donohue said. "He'll tell you what it's really like here."

When Mr. Donohue left them alone, the black player told Lew, "You'd be crazy to come here. There are just a couple of blacks here. You'd be isolated, just like I am. Pick someplace else."

So Lew thanked Mr. Donohue, and said that he had decided on UCLA. Lew and Mr. Donohue parted friends. Lew always respected Mr. Donohue as being a very good coach.

At UCLA, Lew was put on the freshman team. The rules didn't allow him to
play on the varsity until his second year
at school. The whole freshman team was
good. It had some of the best players
from across the United States. It was
almost too easy for the team. They won
every game they played, they even beat
one team by 103 points. And in an inter-
squad match, the freshman team beat
the varsity team of UCLA by 15 points.
The UCLA varsity had been champions
of the whole United States just the year
before.

The coaches could see that Lew
wasn't getting the work-outs that he
needed from the regular games. So they
hired Jay Carty to work out with him.
Jay had starred at Oregon State and now
was working on his advanced degree at
UCLA. Mostly, they played one-on-one
matches. Jay gave Lew a hard time. He

went at Lew, using his knees and elbows. It reminded Lew of the basketball he played at Holy Providence. But it was good toughening practice.

The next year, Lew was on the varsity team, and everybody expected them to win everything, including the national championship. Lew and the other players weren't so sure. They had plenty of team-work to learn, and they worked hard.

In the opening game against Southern California, they could feel the pressure. They were nervous — until they got out onto the court. ULCA won 105 to 90. Lew scored 56 points, a new UCLA record.

The entire season went the way it started. UCLA won every game includ-ing those in the national tournament. Lew finished the season with a 29 point-per-game average. Nobody could stop the UCLA team. If the other team put too many men to guard Lew, he would pass off to the other players. At least one of them was bound to be open for a clear shot at the basket. If the other team didn't guard Lew closely enough, he'd score lots of baskets.

During the summer, Lew went to New York City with other black basketball players to work with children. Here he shows the boys how to hold the ball to make a dunk shot.

UPI

That summer, Lew took a job in Harlem. He and two black players from the New York Knicks basketball team went from playground to playground teaching basketball to young boys. For Lew, it was a wonderful summer.

The next season was smooth sailing too, except that they lost one game by two points. Lew had a bad scratch on one eyeball and couldn't play as well as usual. Off the basketball court, however, some things troubled Lew.

Lew found racial prejudice in California just as he found it in New York. Questions of brotherhood among all men had always been important to Lew. And going all the way from New York to California hadn't changed that.

In looking for answers to these questions, Lew became interested in the Moslem religion. He was beginning to feel that the Moslems had a stronger answer. They taught that there was only one God, and that all men were brothers. To Lew, it seemed that the Moslems cared more about deeds of brotherhood than words. He liked that.

The summer after his junior year was time for the Olympics. Lew was invited to play on the United States' basketball team. After much thought, and after talking it over with his friends, Lew decided not to join the Olympic team. Instead, he went back to his summer job working with the boys in poor New York neighborhoods. Lew spent his time trying to convince poor blacks that they should stay in school and learn how to make a living.

Lew felt the job he did that summer was more important than playing in the Olympics.

Also during the summer, Lew began his formal education in the Moslem religion. He studied at the Sunnite Mosque in Harlem. Later, he decided to join the Moslem religion. And he changed his

Lew (Number 33) takes the rebound out of the hands of Elvin Hayes of Houston during the NCAA semi-finals (March, 1967).

name to Kareem Abdul Jabbar. It means "generous servant of God."

Lew went back to UCLA in the fall. At first he didn't tell any of his friends or teammates about his new name and religion. He was afraid they might be upset. But one night he told them. They weren't upset. They respected the change, and began to call him by his new name, Kareem. Sometimes one of his friends would forget and call him Lew. But Kareem didn't mind. He was still proud of his former name.

In his senior year, the UCLA team went right on winning. They did lose one game. Everybody on the team seemed to be off that night. But the game didn't mean anything. And UCLA won the national championship for the third year in a row.

When Kareem was graduated from

UCLA, he was the number one college basketball player. All the professional teams wanted him. But the Milwaukee team drew the right to offer him a contract. Kareem would rather have played for a New York team. But he liked Milwaukee too.

And Milwaukee liked him. Kareem

Kareem Abdul Jabbar's record in professional basketball 1969-1973

Year	Games played	Field goals tried	Field goals made	Percent	Free throws tried
1969-70	82	1810	938	.52	743
1970-71	82	1843	1063	.58	681
1971-72	81	2019	1159	.57	732
1972-73	76	1773	982	.55	475

Leading scorer — National Basketball Association: 1970-71, 1971-72 immediately turned a team with a poor record into a team fighting for the top. In 1971, he led Milwaukee to its first championship.

From a clumsy, oversized boy, Kareem Abdul Jabbar had grown into a giant of the basketball world, one of the greatest players of all time.

Free throws made	Percent	Total points	Average per game	Rebounds
485	.65	2361	28.8	1190
470	.69	2596	31.7	1311
504	.69	2822	34.8	1346
328	.69	2292	30.2	1224

Bobby Orr

Bobby Orr

YOUNG Bobby Orr wondered what was going on. A stranger had come to his house in Parry Sound, Ontario. The stranger was downstairs in the living room talking to his father. Bobby was sure they were talking about him. And he was curious.

After a while, Bobby's father called him. Bobby came down the stairs and walked shyly into the living room.

"Bobby, this is Mr. Blair. He saw you play last week. He has come all the way from Boston to talk with us."

Bobby shook hands with the stranger.

"I thought you played a great game," Mr. Blair said. "Sorry your team didn't

win the finals."

"Thanks," Bobby said. "It was a close game."

Bobby's hockey team had just played in the all-Ontario Canada Bantam Championship Tournament at Gananoque, Ontario. They had done well enough to reach the finals, but they had lost the last big game, 1-0.

Even though his team had lost the championship, Bobby had won a victory. He had been named Most Valuable Player in the tournament — and he was the youngest, smallest boy on his team!

Bobby played with the Bantam Division of the Parry Sound hockey league. He was only 12 years old, five feet two inches tall, and 110 pounds. Most of the boys his age were in the PeeWee Division. But Bobby played so well that he was asked to play with the older team.

After Mr. Blair left, Bobby's father said, "Well, that was interesting. Blair was at Gananoque scouting for the Boston Bruins hockey team. And Bobby, he thinks you could be a professional player someday."

"Wow!" Bobby said. He could hardly believe it! It seemed that every boy in his hometown played hockey. Every one of them probably dreamed about playing in the professional leagues someday. But this was no dream. Mr. Blair was a real professional scout, and he had just said that he — Bobby Orr — might have a future in hockey!

Bobby could see that his father was pleased too. He knew his father had once thought about being a professional hockey player himself. When Mr. Orr was younger, he had been invited to try-out with the Boston Bruins. But that was in 1942, during World War II, and he had joined the Canadian Navy instead.

After the war, Bobby's father settled down to raise his family. But Bobby's father often thought about professional hockey and what he might have done if there hadn't been a war.

It seemed to Bobby that hockey had always been important to his family. His older brother played in the Parry Sound

league. And his two sisters were loyal fans.

Bobby had been skating since he could remember. He must have been just four years old when he learned to skate out on the frozen river. He and other boys from town used to play "shinny." One boy would get the puck, then see how long he could keep it away from all the others. It was a free-for-all. Only a good skater could keep the puck for very long.

Even in those days, Bobby could remember his father stopping to watch and to cheer him on.

Later, Bobby joined the children's leagues. He played in the indoor rink at

the community center. First, there was Minor Squirt for five- and six-year-olds, then Squirt and PeeWee. Bobby's father always came to the games when he could.

Mr. Orr was proud of his son. Now he was thrilled to think that he might one day watch Bobby play in professional games.

The next day, Bobby's father came home from work even more excited. "I guess Boston is really serious," he told Bobby's mother. "They gave our community center some money for the indoor ice rink."

Ice hockey and the chance to play professional was all the talk at the Orr house for several weeks. But then spring came. The ice melted and everybody forgot about hockey for a while.

Late the next fall, Mr. Blair came back to Parry Sound. And he brought with him the whole Kingston Frontenac team that he was managing. The Frontenacs were a minor league professional team owned by the Boston major league club.

The Frontenacs put on an exhibition at the community center for the whole town. While Mr. Blair was in town, he stopped to visit the Orr family and spent a few hours talking hockey with Bobby's father.

Three or four more times during the winter season, Mr. Blair came through Parry Sound with the Frontenacs. Everybody thought that was very unusual because Parry Sound was a small town and out of the way. No team had ever taken such an interest in the town before.

Bobby was still playing Bantam Division and having fun. That hockey season seemed to go by in a flash. Bobby's team had a so-so season, but Bobby enjoyed playing anyhow. He played defenseman. He liked the position because he was always in the middle of the action. When the other team had the puck, he had to check the rushes of the other team and help protect his goal.

But Bobby was good on offense too. When his team had the puck, he could switch to offense and race up the ice to shoot for a goal. And he was always the top scorer. He was a fast enough skater to do both jobs well.

During the summer, Mr. Blair stopped by again to see Bobby's father. This time he was alone. The two men had a long talk. Mr. Blair wanted Bobby to attend tryout camp at Niagara Falls. At first, Bobby's father didn't like the idea. It was so far from home and Bobby was still young. But Mr. Blair said that another boy from Parry Sound was planning to go. And Mr. Blair promised to look after Bobby. Bobby's father finally said yes.

Bobby was excited. It was a real adventure. About 70 boys, mostly from Ontario and Quebec, came to the try-out camp for a week. They went to classes to learn plays. They learned tips on passing and stick-handling. They learned checking and how to defend against power plays. They learned about every part of the game. After classes, they played hockey. And that's what the boys liked the best.

At the end of the week, they had a final round of games. Bobby's father drove over to Niagara Falls to watch.

"Mr. Blair tells me you've done real well," Bobby's father told him. "And I think so too. You looked good in the action I saw."

Right then and there, Mr. Blair wanted to sign Bobby to play semi-pro Junior A hockey. He asked Bobby's father to give his permission. But Bobby's father said he wanted to talk it over with his wife first.

So Bobby and his father drove home to talk it over. Mr. Blair followed close behind. The next day, hockey was the big subject at the Orr home. Mr. Blair argued that Bobby should play Junior A hockey so that he could keep getting better. The tougher competition would help him improve. But Bobby's mother didn't like the idea.

To play Junior A hockey, Bobby would have to play with the Oshawa Generals, and Oshawa was a suburb of Toronto, 150 miles from Parry Sound. Bobby's mother didn't want Bobby to be away from home. After all, he was only 14 years old.

Finally, they reached an agreement. Bobby would play with the Oshawa Generals, but only on weekends. He would stay at home with his family during the week and his father would drive him back and forth from Parry Sound to Oshawa for the weekend games.

The plan didn't work out very well. For one thing, Bobby wasn't able to practice with the team during the week. And his father had to spend so much time driving that he hardly ever saw the rest of his family on weekends.

Bobby's teammates were upset too. They felt that Bobby was getting special favors. But when they saw how well Bobby played, the other boys were glad he was on their team. That year Bobby scored 13 goals while playing good defense, and he was named to the all-star team, second-string.

The next season, Bobby was 15 years old. His mother agreed to let him live with a family in Oshawa and go to high school there.

Bobby was getting better and better as a hockey player. His stick-handling was sharper. His passing game was crisper. And the chance to practice regularly with his teammates helped too. That year he scored 30 goals as a defenseman, a new league record. All the coaches in the league voted him all-star defenseman, first team.

Bobby was becoming famous. Newspapers printed stories about him. And the next year, his picture was printed on the front cover of *Maclean's Magazine*, the largest magazine in Canada. All this attention made Bobby feel shy. When someone asked him what he thought of the stories, he answered, "I try not to read them or think about them."

All the attention Bobby was getting in the newspapers made some of the players in the league jealous. Hockey is a rough game. And there are lots of ways a jealous player can work out his feelings.

MACLEAN'S 15¢

Canada's National Magazine February 20 1965

The shameful plight of half a million Canadian families:

OUR INVISIBLE POOR

How hockey's hottest 16-year-old is groomed for stardom

Bobby Orr: a fan's-eye view. Has Boston captured the NHL's next super-star?

Bobby could tell that some of the players were checking him harder and harder. Once in a while, he would feel a hockey stick jammed into his ribs. Or he would have to duck a hockey stick aimed at his head.

Bobby always tried to play hard and clean. But he knew he couldn't back away, either. So he went on playing the best he could. And he played great hockey. The next year, he broke the record again with 34 goals and 59 assists. And the following year, he broke the record for the third year in a row, scoring 37 goals and 60 assists.

Bobby was 18 years old now, old enough to sign a regular contract with a professional team. Because Boston had signed him to play Junior A hockey, they had first rights by league rules. All the newspaper and magazine stories over the years had made Bobby famous even though he was young. All this was good for the Boston Bruins team. They used this buildup of Bobby to keep the fans interested in the team. And they needed all the help they could get. The Boston Bruins had been playing poorly for several years.

When it came to contract time, the Boston team sent Hap Emms to get a contract signed. He met with Bobby's father and offered the standard contract, a salary of $8,000.

But Bobby's father thought that Bobby was worth more than that. Bobby was more than just a good player. He was a great player. The team really needed him. And Mr. Orr knew that the Boston fans were eagerly waiting to see Bobby in a Boston uniform next year. If Boston wanted Bobby so much, they should pay him more money.

Finally, Bobby's father called a lawyer

to help Bobby get the best possible contract. This lawyer was known for working out good contracts for hockey players.

Back and forth went the offers and counter-offers. Finally, after days of talks, an agreement was reached. Bobby signed for over $50,000. Bobby had one of the best contracts ever signed by a rookie. And Boston had one of the best rookies ever signed.

Boston held their training camp for the 1966 season at London, Ontario. It opened in September. Bobby was excited and a little scared. He was like most rookies. He didn't know what to expect.

He was assigned to a room. He put his things away and tried to settle down. But he was so nervous he couldn't stay still. He walked around town. He looked in store windows. Practice wasn't supposed to start for a couple of hours, but finally he couldn't stand it. He decided to get to the rink early and skate his nervousness off.

When Bobby got to the locker room, he was surprised. He thought he would be the only one there. But he was the last to arrive. The whole team was in the locker room, and there was a blanket spread out on the locker-room floor.

"What's that for?" Bobby asked.

"It's our magic blanket," answered one of the players. "It's the only one like it in the world."

"Lie down on it," another said. "And see what marvelous tricks it can do. It can even lift you right into the air."

That sounded crazy to Bobby. But just to prove how silly it was, Bobby lay down in the center and folded his arms. "OK," he said. "Let's see it do some magic."

Suddenly, a couple of the players jumped on Bobby and rolled him up into the blanket. He was wrapped so well he couldn't move. Then they got out a razor and began to shave Bobby's head. When they were finished, Bobby was absolutely bald.

Bobby had received the initiation into the team. His teammates had been waiting to do this ever since he had arrived.

Everybody laughed. Bobby laughed too when he looked in the mirror. He didn't look like one of the highest-paid new stars in professional hockey. He looked more like a chicken without its feathers.

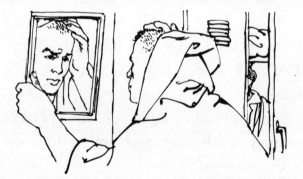

Now Bobby was really a member of the Boston Bruins. It seemed as if his whole life had been moving toward this moment, from the time he was a little boy playing "shinny" on the frozen river in Parry Sound. Everything that had happened in his life was real, yet it was all as wonderful as a dream.

This was the beginning of a new life for Bobby Orr. And it was a new start for the Boston Bruins hockey team. Bobby was off on a bright career that would earn him the highest standing in the hockey world. He would receive many trophies and awards for his skill as defenseman. He would be called the greatest defenseman who ever played, and perhaps the greatest hockey player who ever lived.

And, for the Boston Bruins, it was a turning point when Bobby joined the team. After many years of poor play and

Bobby (Number 4) whizzes by and takes the puck. That season (1966-67) he won a trophy as the best rookie of the year.

even poorer records, the Boston team was on the road up toward the highest goal in hockey, the Stanley Cup. And it was Bobby Orr who would lead them there in 1970 and again in 1972. In 1970, Bobby scored 33 goals and 87 assists for a total of 120 points — 56 points more than any defenseman had ever scored before.

And the next year he scored 139 points. Bobby has many more seasons of hockey ahead of him. Who knows what greater records he'll set!

Bobby Orr's record in professional hockey
1966-1973

Year	Games played	Goals	Assists	Total points
1966-67	73	13	28	41
*1967-68	46	11	20	31
1968-69	76	21	43	64
1969-70	76	33	87	120
1970-71	78	37	102	139
1971-72	76	37	80	117
1972-73	63	29	72	101

Hart Trophy — for most valuable player: 1969-70, 1970-71, 1971-72

Norris Trophy — for best defenseman: 1967-68, 1968-69, 1969-70, 1970-71, 1971-72, 1972-73

Calder Trophy — for best rookie: 1966-67

Art Ross Trophy — for most scoring points 1969-70 (Only time given to a defenseman)

*Knee injury made Bobby miss almost half the games.